P9-DVT-259

Grizzly Bears

by Molly Kolpin

Consultant:
Frank T. van Manen
Research Ecologist
U.S. Geological Survey
Leetown Science Center

CAPSTONE PRESS
a capstone imprint

First Facts is published by Capstone Press,
151 Good Counsel Drive, P.O. Box 669, Mankato, Minnesota 56002.
www.capstonepub.com

Books published by Capstone Press are manufactured with paper
containing at least 10 percent post-consumer waste.

Library of Congress Cataloging-in-Publication Data
Kolpin, Molly.
  Grizzly bears / by Molly Kolpin.
    p. cm. — (First facts. Bears)
  Includes bibliographical references and index.
  Summary: "Discusses grizzly bears, including their physical features, habitat, range,
and life cycle"—Provided by publisher.
  ISBN 978-1-4296-6129-4 (library binding)
  ISBN 978-1-4296-7187-3 (paperback)
  1. Grizzly bear—Juvenile literature. I. Title.
  QL737.C27K65 2012
  599.784—dc22   2011001343

Editorial Credits

Christine Peterson, editor; Kyle Grenz, designer; Laura Manthe, production specialist

Photo Credits

Alamy: Jeff Mondragon, 10, Laura Romin & Larry Dalton, 13, Photoshot Holding Ltd,
5, WILDLIFE GmbH, 20; Corel, 9; Getty Images Inc.: Photolibrary/Daniel Cox, 16;
Shutterstock: Antoni Murcia, 1, 19, Florian Andronache, cover, JKlingebiel, 6, Kane513,
15, Rick Parsons, 21

Artistic Effects

Shutterstock: Andrejs Pidjass, basel101658

Essential content terms are **bold** and are defined at the bottom of the spread where they
first appear.

Printed in the United States of America in North Mankato, Minnesota.
032011   006110CGF11

Table of Contents

Large and in Charge

Grizzly bears are one of the most powerful **mammals** in North America. They are also one of the largest. These huge, towering bears are 5 to 8 feet (1.5 to 2.4 meters) long. They stand up to 5 feet (1.5 m) tall at the shoulders. Grizzlies can weigh more than 800 pounds (363 kilograms).

Fact!
A grizzly's thick, stiff fur can be tan or brown.

mammal—a warm-blooded animal that has a backbone and breathes air

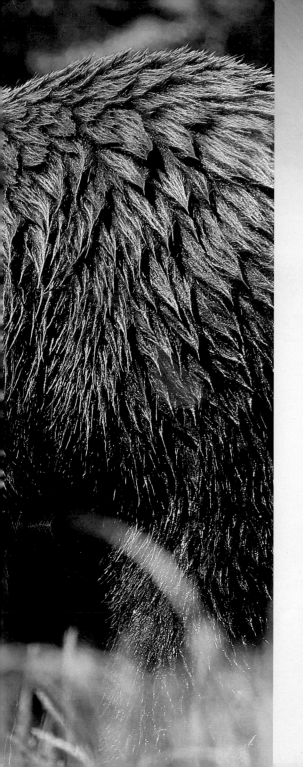

Extra Strength

Grizzlies have a hump of muscle between their shoulders. This hump gives a grizzly extra strength and power. These bears can take down animals that outweigh them by hundreds of pounds.

Fact!
Most grizzlies don't bother people. But they may attack to defend their cubs.

The Great Outdoors

Grizzlies are brown bears. They are only called grizzlies in North America. Grizzlies roam across northwestern United States and western Canada. They live near rivers or streams in home **ranges.**

Grizzly Range in yellow

Arctic Ocean

Pacific Ocean

Atlantic Ocean

Indian Ocean

Antarctic Ocean

N W E S

Grizzly bears like to be alone. They rub trees to spread their **scent**. The scent marks a grizzly's area and keeps other bears away.

range—an area where an animal mostly lives
scent—the odor or smell of something

Fact!
Grizzly bears can smell prey from 3 miles (4.8 km) away!

Sharp Senses

Grizzlies use their sharp sense of smell to find **prey**. They can smell animals in **burrows**. For larger meals, grizzlies hunt young elk or moose.

In summer grizzlies eat salmon. They strike down the fish with their paws. Grizzlies can even catch a fish in midair.

prey—an animal hunted by another animal for food
burrow—a tunnel or hole in the ground where an animal lives

Packing on the Pounds

Grizzlies also eat plants. They snack on nuts, berries, and leaves. Grizzlies dig up roots with their sharp claws. They also dig up small mammals that live underground.

In late summer and fall, a grizzly may eat nonstop for 20 hours a day. All this eating helps grizzlies fatten up for winter.

claws

13

Winter Snooze

When winter comes, a grizzly digs a den in a hillside. It piles up dry leaves for a bed. The bear spends the next four to six months **hibernating** in its cozy hideout.

hibernate—to spend the winter in a deep sleep

Life Cycle of a Grizzly Bear

Newborn—At birth, cubs have no fur and cannot see.

Young—Grizzlies stay with their mothers
for two or three years.

grizzly cubs

Adult—Grizzlies are fully grown by age 10.

Young Grizzlies

Adult grizzlies **mate** in late spring. Cubs are born in January or February. Usually two cubs are born at a time. At birth, cubs are the size of small rats.

Cubs spend their first four months drinking their mother's milk. They keep warm in their mother's den. In spring, a mother bear leads her cubs out of their winter home.

mate—to join together to produce young

Don't Mess with Mama

A mother grizzly teaches her cubs how to survive in the wild. She also protects them from danger. If an enemy is near, she sends her cubs up a tree. Then she charges the enemy. Female grizzlies can **sprint** up to 30 miles (48 km) per hour.

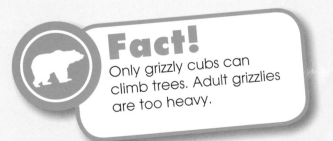

Fact!
Only grizzly cubs can climb trees. Adult grizzlies are too heavy.

sprint—to run fast for a short distance

Growing Strong

Grizzlies grow most during the first two years of life. They can gain up to 200 pounds (91 km). Grizzlies are adults at age 5. In the wild, grizzlies can live to be 30 years old.

Amazing but True!

Grizzlies are one of the world's strongest animals. They can kill large prey with one swipe of a paw. Their powerful jaws and claws can tear apart logs like toys. One grizzly even bit through a cast iron skillet!

Glossary

burrow (BUHR-oh)—a tunnel or hole in the ground where an animal lives

hibernate (HYE-bur-nate)—to spend the winter in a deep sleep

mammal (MAM-uhl)—a warm-blooded animal that has a backbone and breathes air

mate (MATE)—to join together to produce young

prey (PRAY)—an animal hunted by another animal for food

range (RAYNJ)—an area where an animal mostly lives

scent (SENT)—the odor or smell of something

sprint (SPRINT)—to run fast for a short distance

Read More

Barner, Bob. *Bears! Bears! Bears!* San Francisco: Chronicle Books, 2010.

Dineen, Jacqueline. *Grizzly Bears.* Amazing Animals. New York: Weigl, 2010.

Shea, Therese. *Grizzly Bears.* Animals that Live in the Tundra. New York: Gareth Stevens Pub., 2011.

Smith, Lucy Sackett. *Grizzly Bears: Fierce Hunters.* Mighty Mammals. New York: PowerKids Press, 2010.

Internet Sites

FactHound offers a safe, fun way to find Internet sites related to this book. All of the sites on FactHound have been researched by our staff.

Here's all you do:

Visit *www.facthound.com*

Type in this code: 9781429661294

 Super-cool stuff! Check out projects, games and lots more at **www.capstonekids.com**

Index